THE NEW YORKER
BOOK OF TEACHER CARTOONS

THE NEW YORKER
BOOK OF TEACHER CARTOONS

EDITED BY ROBERT MANKOFF

BLOOMBERG PRESS

NEW YORK

PUBLISHED BY BLOOMBERG PRESS

To purchase framed prints of cartoons or to license cartoons for use in periodicals, Web sites, or other media, please contact CARTOONBANK.COM, a New Yorker Magazine company, at 28 Wells Avenue, Building #3, 4th Floor, Yonkers, NY 10701, Tel: 800-897-TOON, or (914) 478-5527, Fax: (914) 478-5604, e-mail: toon@cartoonbank.com, Web: www.cartoonbank.com.

Books are available for bulk purchases at special discounts. Special editions or book excerpts can also be created to specifications. For information, please write: Special Markets Department, Bloomberg Press.

First edition published 2006
3 5 7 9 10 8 6 4 2
Printed in Mexico

ISBN-13: 978-1-57660-130-3

The Library of Congress has cataloged the earlier printing as follows:

The New Yorker book of teacher cartoons / edited by Robert Mankoff.--1st ed.
    p. cm.
  Includes index.
  ISBN 1-57660-130-7 (alk. paper)
  1. Teachers--Caricatures and cartoons. 2. Students--Caricatures and cartoons. 3. American wit and humor, Pictorial. 4. New Yorker (New York, N.Y. : 1925) I. Title: Book of teacher cartoons. II. Mankoff, Robert. III. New Yorker (New York, N.Y. : 1925)

NC1428.N47 2006
741.5'6973--dc22   2006040784

THE
NEW YORKER
BOOK OF TEACHER CARTOONS

"Mrs. Hammond! I'd know you anywhere from
little Billy's portrait of you."

"'GameBoy: A Memoir of Addiction,' by Ronald Markowitz."

THE BERLITZ GUIDE TO PARENT-TEACHER CONFERENCES

TEACHERESE	ENGLISH
Marches to a different drummer.	Nuts.
Needs to brush up on his people skills.	Homicidal.
Creative.	None too bright
Very creative.	A moron, actually.
She's a riot!	I can't stand her.
He's doing just fine.	What's your kid's name again?

R.Chast

"Please, Ms. Sweeney, may I ask where you're going with all this?"

"*Where do you get off saying my kid is grade level?*"

THE FIRST DAY BACK

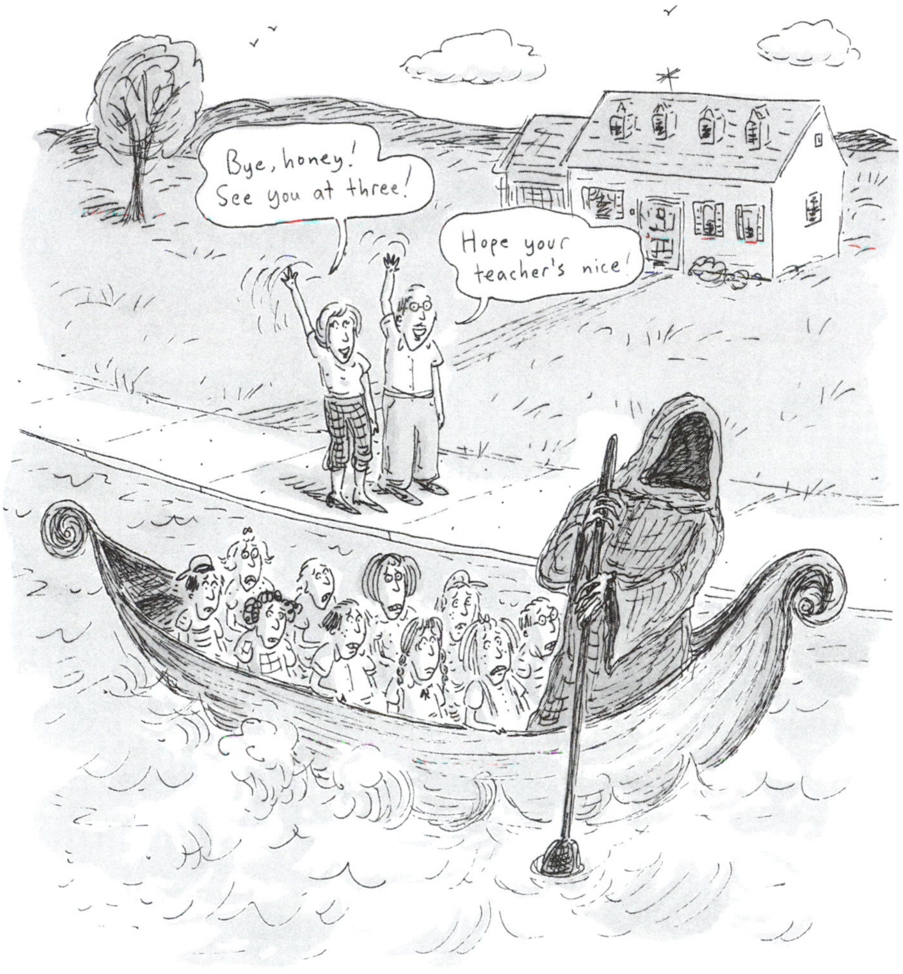
Bye, honey!
See you at three!
Hope your teacher's nice!

"So, what are we aiming for, Timmy—the Nobel Prize or 'Inspected by No. 7'?"

"Mrs. Minton, there's no such thing as a bad boy. Hostile, perhaps. Aggressive, recalcitrant, destructive, even sadistic. But not <u>bad</u>."

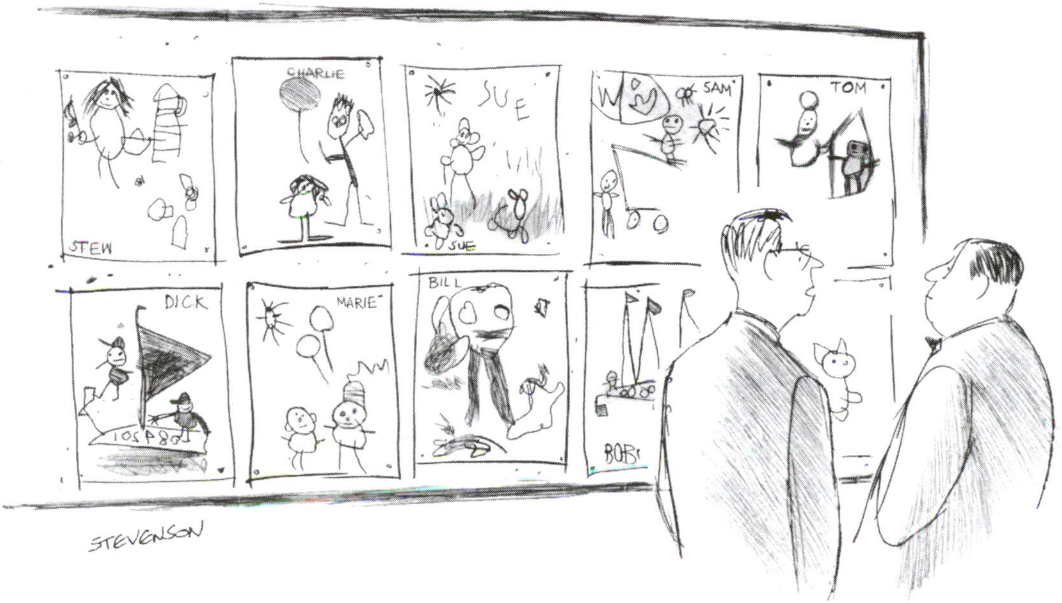
CHARLIE
SUE
SAM
TOM
STEW
SUE
DICK
MARIE
BILL
BOB
STEVENSON

"Which is yours?"

"No one's last words were 'I wish I'd done more homework.'"

"*Unfortunately, all evidence of your son's intelligence is purely anecdotal.*"

"This is Henderson, speaking for Miss Gordy's second-grade ad-hoc students'
committee. Here's a list of our demands."

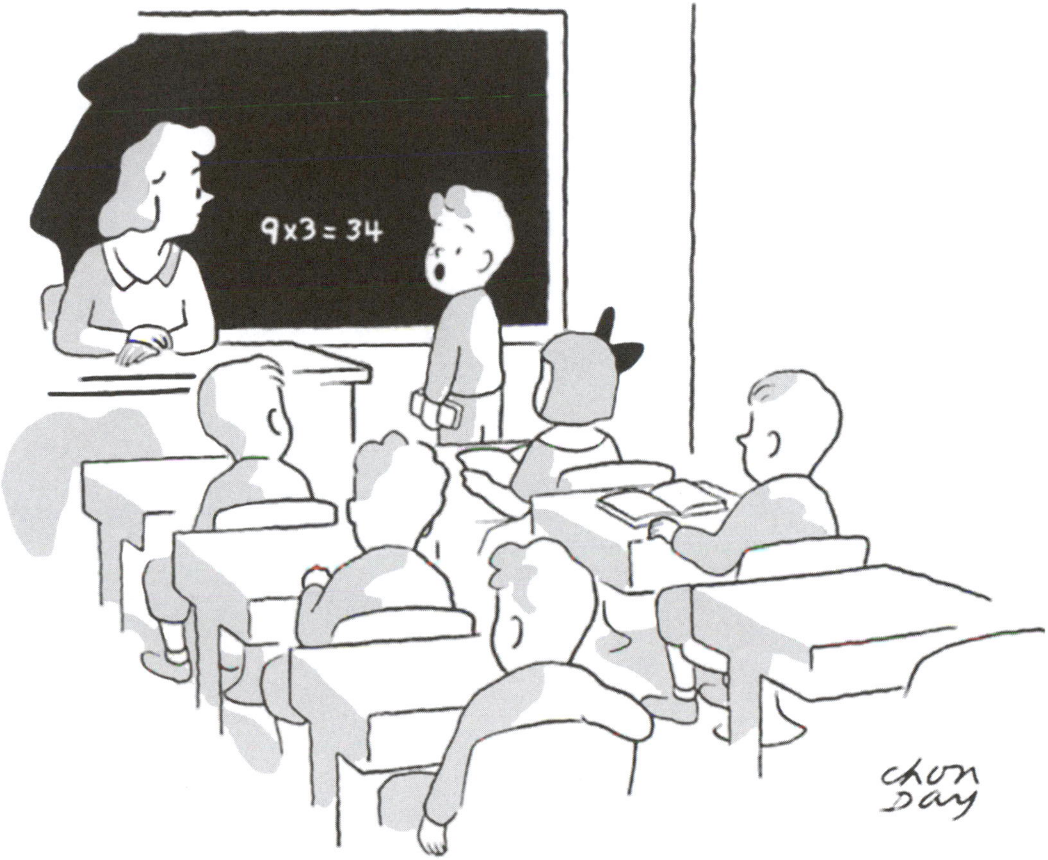
9x3 = 34
CHON DAY

"Am I warm?"

"*My parents didn't write it—they just tweaked it.*"

*"Thompson, how about you and Miss Hobson shaking hands,
and let's see if we can't make a fresh start."*

"May I remind you, Jensen, that teacher evaluation by
the group has yet to be approved."

"I see trouble with algebra."

"In a nutshell, Mrs. Turner, either your son is making an unusually fine adjustment to his lack of ability or else he just doesn't give a damn."

"*Your armies have deserted you, you have been wounded unto death. Now make me* feel *it!*"

"But, Eugene, it's not enough to be gifted. We've got to
_do_ something with our gift."

"Miss Peterson, may I go home? I can't assimilate any more data today."

"I'm sorry, Timmy, but you are wrong. You are terribly, terribly wrong."

"We've created a safe, nonjudgemental environment that will
leave your child ill-prepared for real-life."

"So __what__ if the Applebaum kid thinks you're a down trip? The rest of your students gave you terrific report cards."

"*Thank you for coming. The talks were forthright and useful, and provided an excellent climate in which to resolve our remaining differences.*"

"Oh no, not homework again."

"So what if he paid a classmate to do
his homework—it was his own allowance."

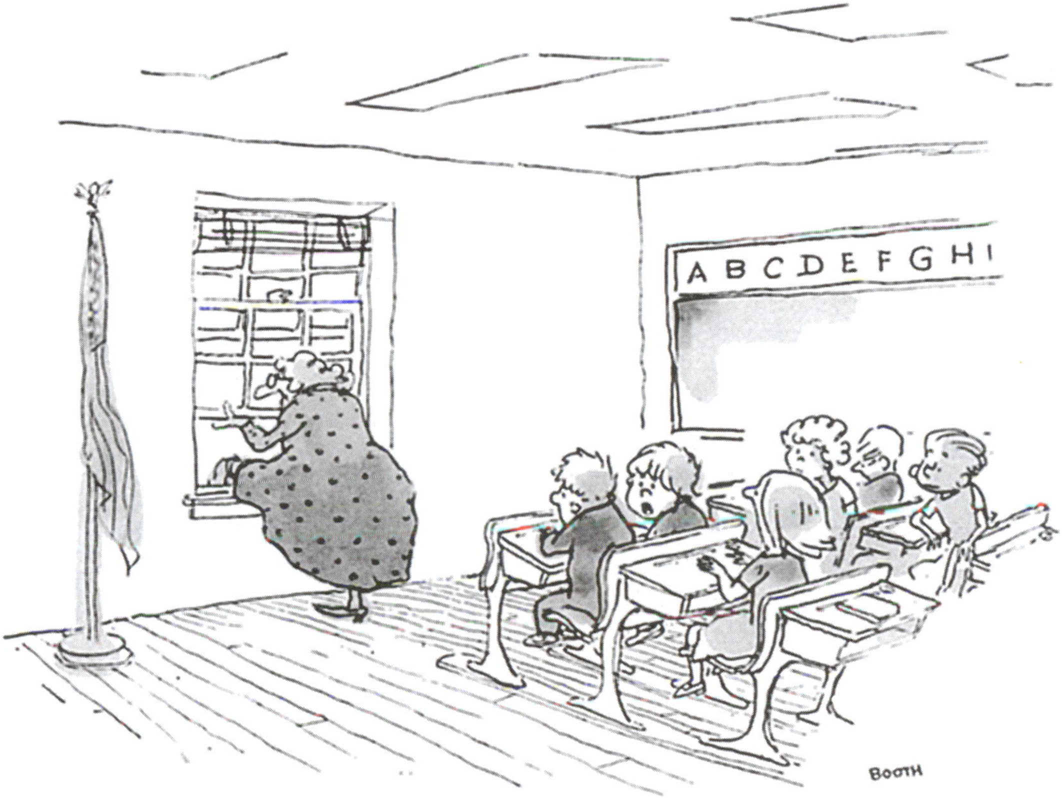
A B C D E F G H I
BOOTH

"Teacher burnout."

"All right, children, who wants to open our discussion of the Papa Bear's sense of rage? Tommy?"

"'What I Did on My Summer Vacation,' by special
arrangement with the New Jersey State Police."

CAT

"To sum up . . ."

"He's very quick with an answer. But it's never the right one."

THE END OF INNOCENCE

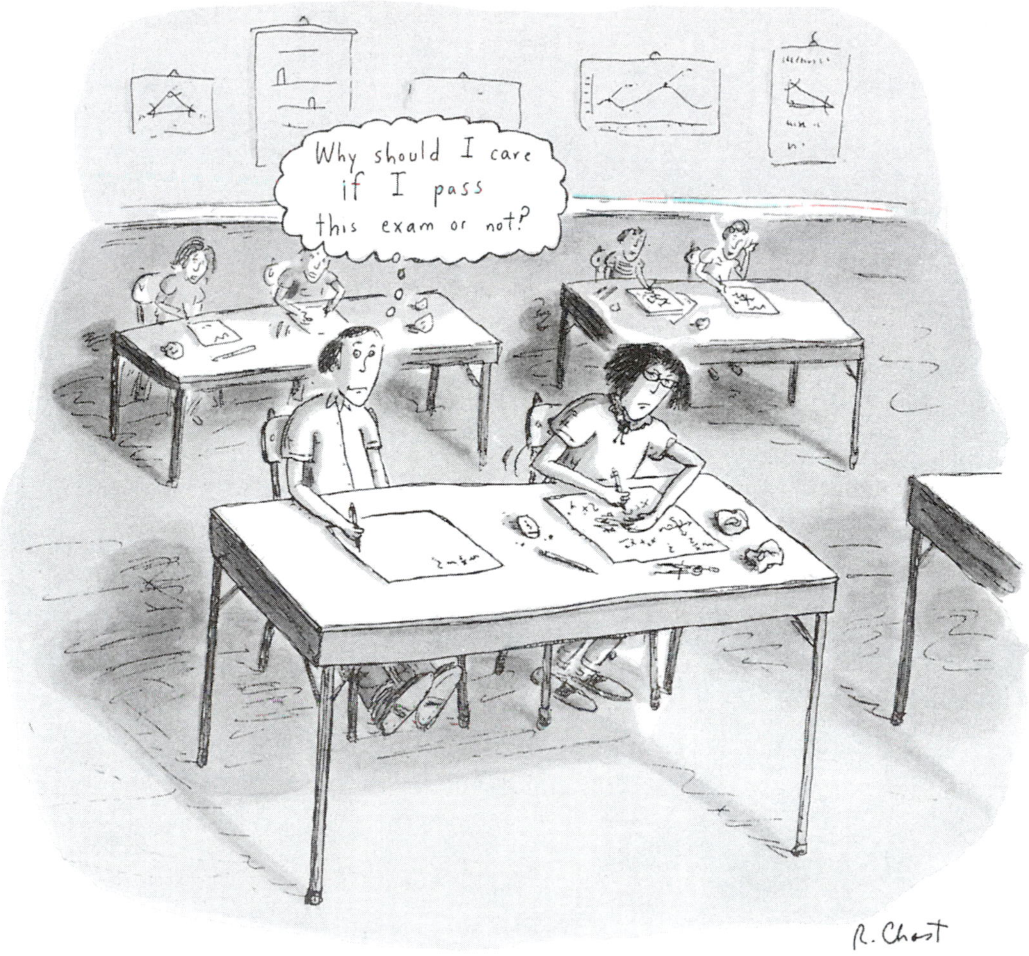
Why should I care if I pass this exam or not?
R. Chast

"*That is the correct answer, Billy, but I'm afraid you don't win anything for it.*"

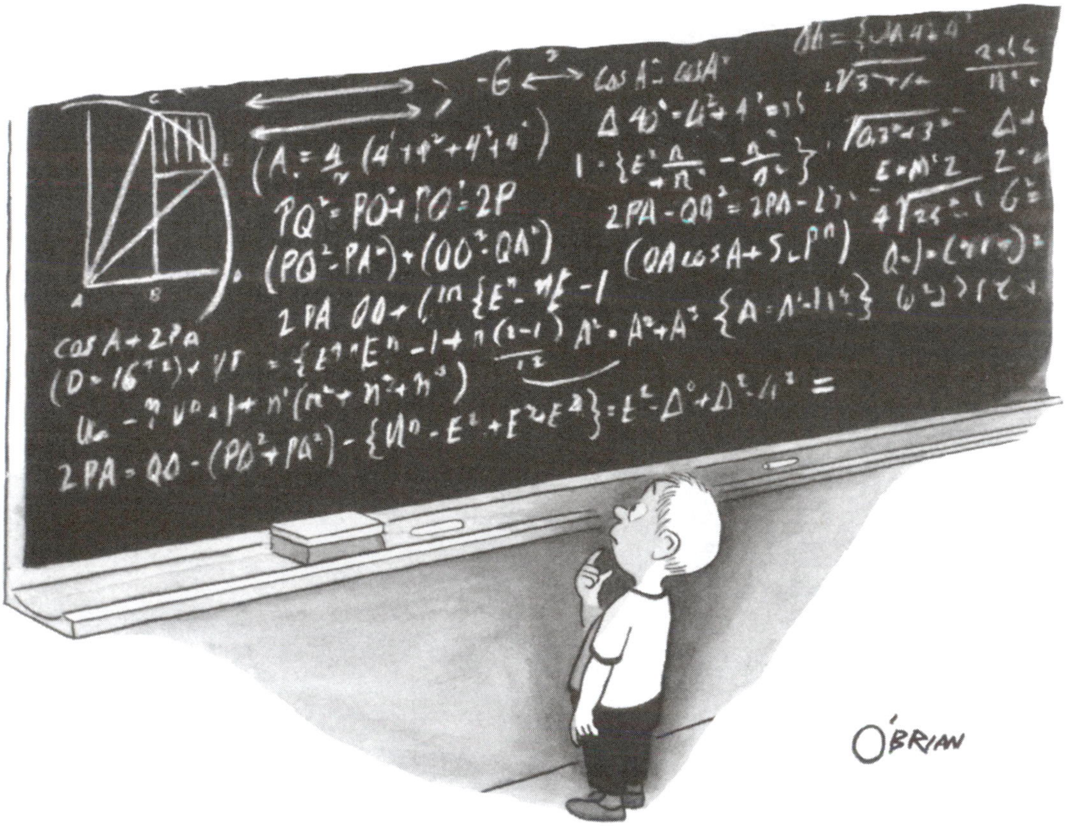
O'BRIAN

"Think!"

"*If I may, Mr. Perlmutter, I'd like to answer your question <u>with</u> a question.*"

"But, sweetie, children are the backbone of our educational system."

"Sarah's grades are excellent. She got A+ in 'Yogi Berra: Philosopher or Fall Guy?,'
A in 'Dollars and Scents: An Analysis of Post-Vietnam Perfume Advertising,' A− in 'The
Final Four as Last Judgment: The N.C.A.A. Tournament from a Religious Perspective,' and
A in 'The American Garage Sale: Its Origins, Cultural Implications, and Future.'"

"But is showing you this toy and telling about it the whole story?
Let's take a look at its sales record, as illustrated by this chart,
which compares it with other toys in its price class."

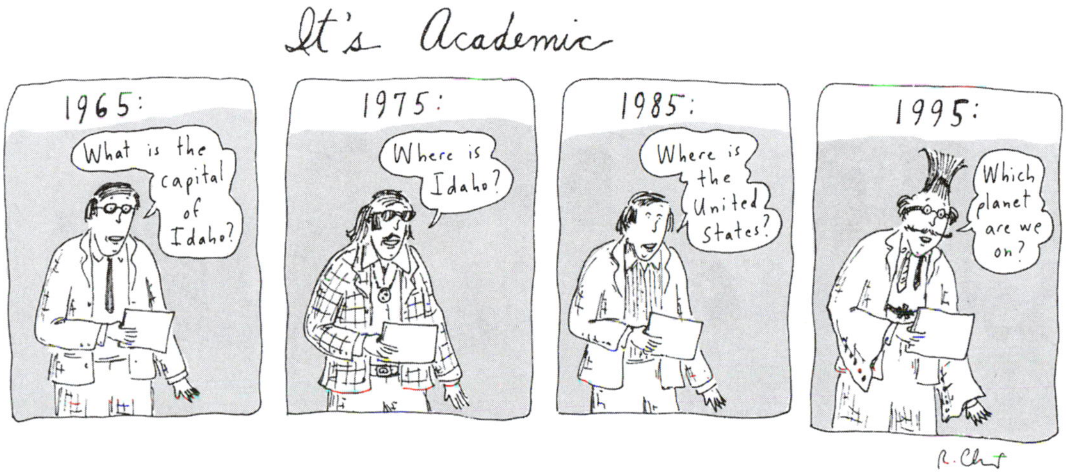
It's Academic
1965:
What is the capital of Idaho?
1975:
Where is Idaho?
1985:
Where is the United States?
1995:
Which planet are we on?
R. Chast

REPORT CARD

Don Diego Vega
Grade III / Mrs. Martinez

Subject	Grade
Spanish	C-
Social Studies	C-
Arithmetic	D
Earth Science	C-
Reading	D
Drawing I	C-
Fencing	A+

Comments: I'm sure that with a little more "toil" and a little less "foil" Don Diego's grades will be on a level with the rest of the class. Mrs. Martinez

Shanahan

THE MARKS OF ZORRO

"A note of warning: The following report may contain material not suitable for the squeamish."

"Miss Jones, may I go home and watch television?"

"*You will like Mr. Woofard. He has an attention-deficit disorder.*"

"*We teach them that the world can be an unpredictable, dangerous, and sometimes frightening place, while being careful not to spoil their lovely innocence. It's tricky.*"

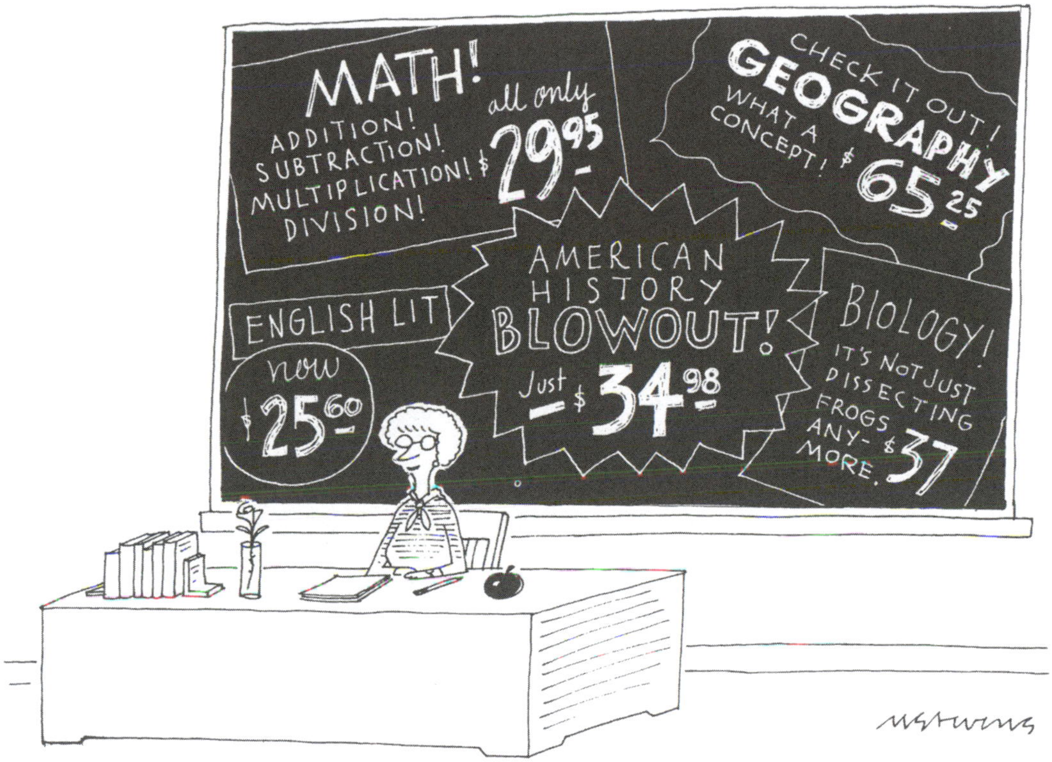
MATH!
ADDITION!
SUBTRACTION!
MULTIPLICATION!
DIVISION!
all only
$29.95
CHECK IT OUT!
GEOGRAPHY
WHAT A CONCEPT!
$65.25
AMERICAN HISTORY
BLOWOUT!
Just $34.98
ENGLISH LIT
now
$25.60
BIOLOGY!
IT'S NOT JUST DISSECTING FROGS ANY-MORE.
$37

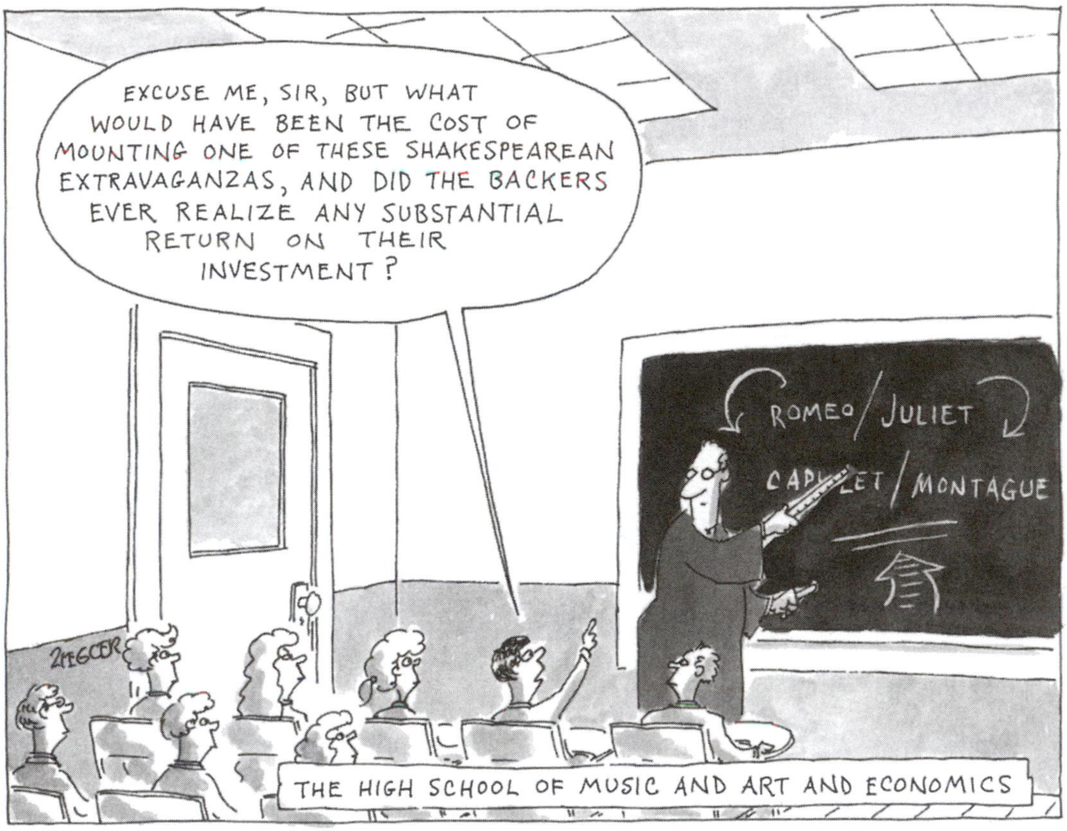
EXCUSE ME, SIR, BUT WHAT WOULD HAVE BEEN THE COST OF MOUNTING ONE OF THESE SHAKESPEAREAN EXTRAVAGANZAS, AND DID THE BACKERS EVER REALIZE ANY SUBSTANTIAL RETURN ON THEIR INVESTMENT?
ROMEO / JULIET
MONTAGUE
ZIEGLER
THE HIGH SCHOOL OF MUSIC AND ART AND ECONOMICS

"The dog ate my homework."

"'Give me liberty or give me death.' Now, what kind of person
would say something like that?"

"My name is Mr. Collins. I'll be teaching you English literature, and I'm armed."

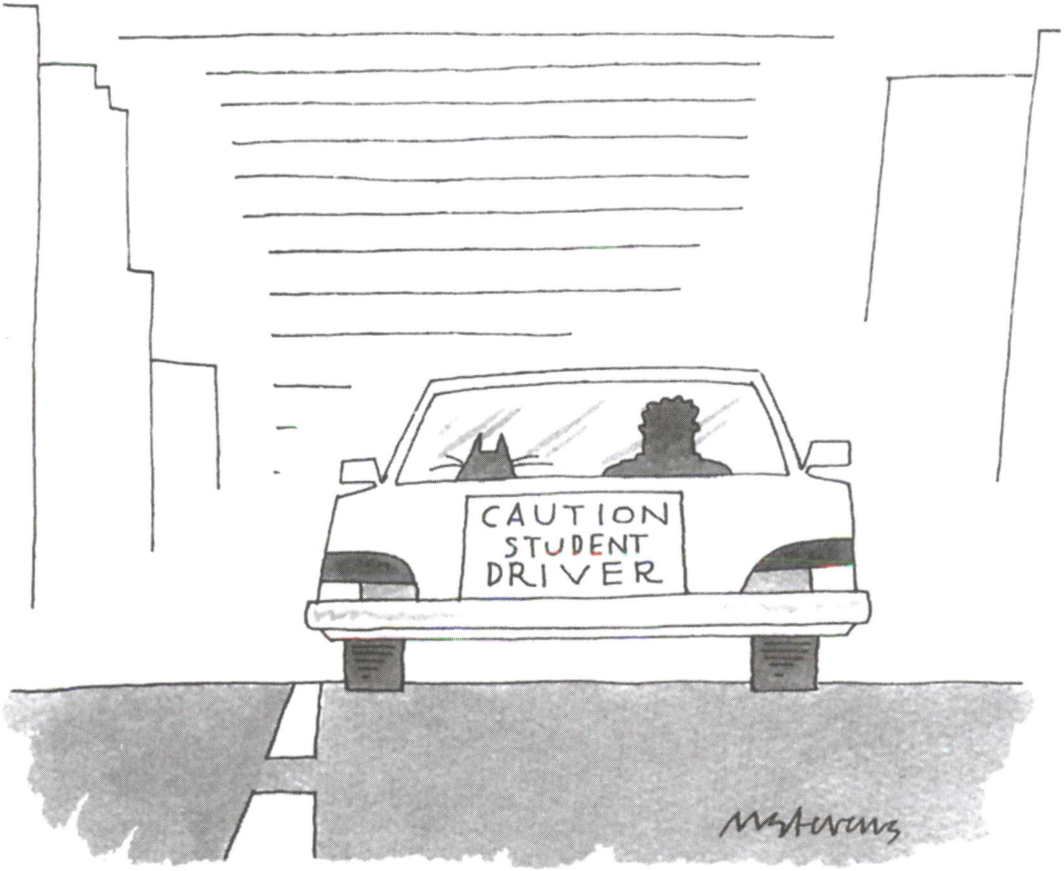
CAUTION
STUDENT
DRIVER

"Oh, yes, indeed. We all keep a sharp eye out for those little
clues that seem to whisper 'law' or 'medicine.'"

"I'm sorry, Mr. Landis, would you repeat the question? I was lost in prayer."

"Now you're probably all asking yourselves, 'Why must I learn to read and write?'"

"Today we're going to learn how to deal with rejection."

"I don't have an answer, but you've sure given me a lot to think about."

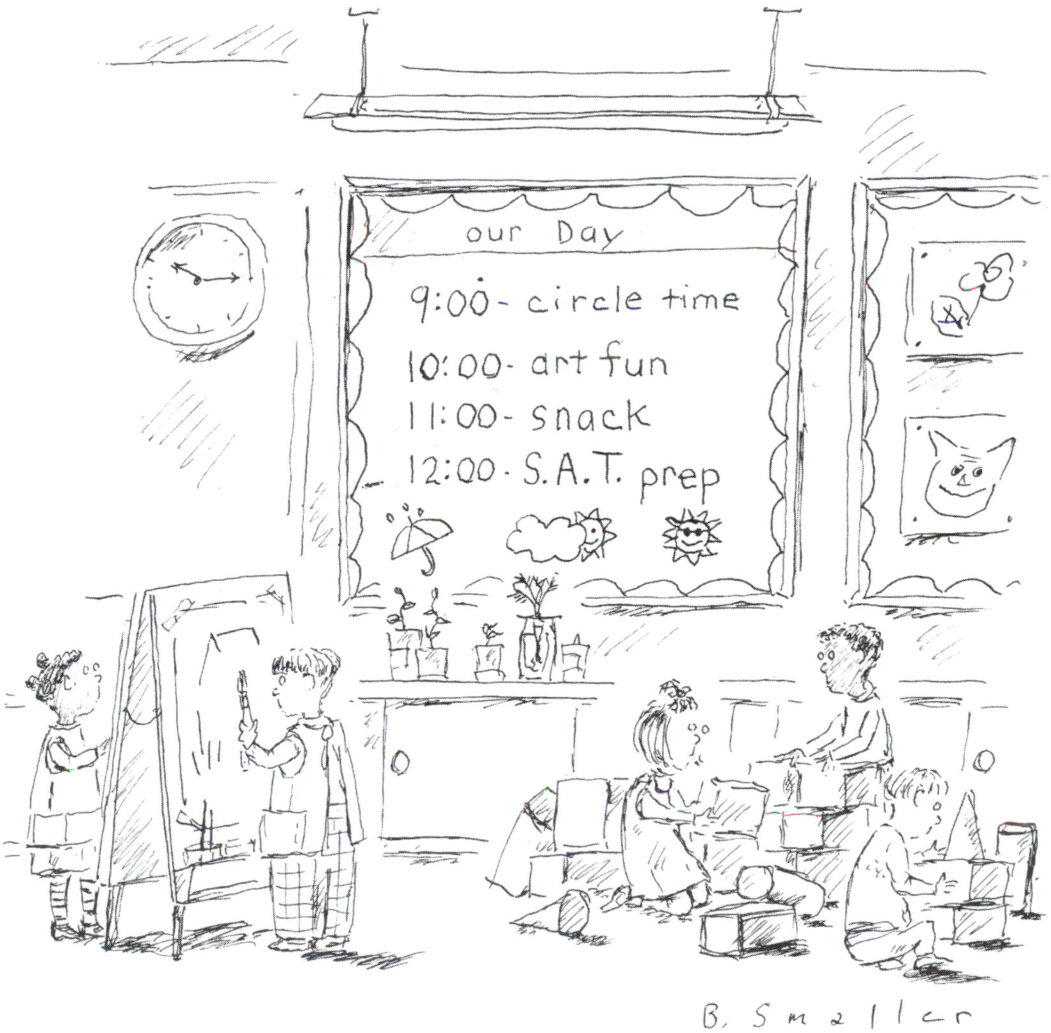
our Day
9:00- circle time
10:00- art fun
11:00- snack
12:00- S.A.T. prep
B. Smaller

"Jason is cute as a bug, but he sure is one thickheaded little sucker."

"I hope you realize that I'm the one who has to write about this stupid vacation next fall."

"Big deal, an A in math. That would be a D in any other country."

"A lot of homework?"

DECONSTRUCTING LUNCH

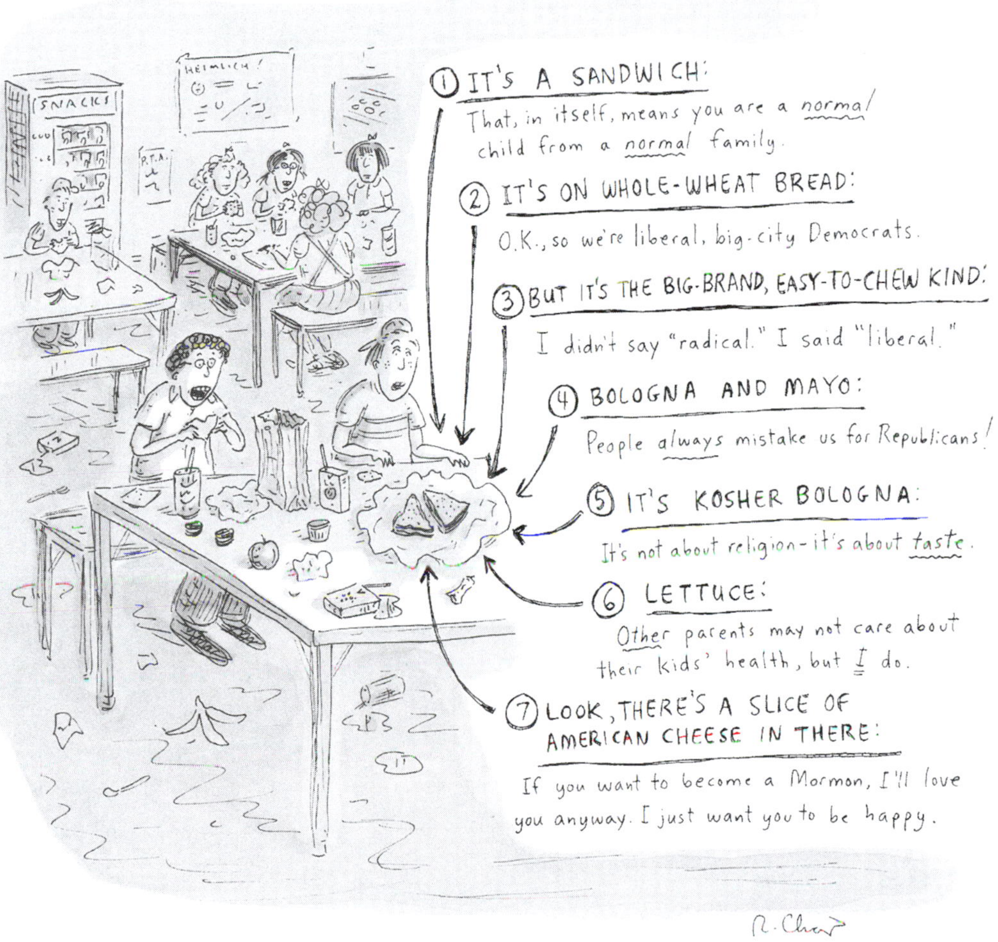

SNACKS
HEIMLICH!
P.T.A.
① IT'S A SANDWICH:
That, in itself, means you are a normal child from a normal family.
② IT'S ON WHOLE-WHEAT BREAD:
O.K., so we're liberal, big-city Democrats.
③ BUT IT'S THE BIG-BRAND, EASY-TO-CHEW KIND:
I didn't say "radical." I said "liberal."
④ BOLOGNA AND MAYO:
People always mistake us for Republicans!
⑤ IT'S KOSHER BOLOGNA:
It's not about religion - it's about taste.
⑥ LETTUCE:
Other parents may not care about their kids' health, but I do.
⑦ LOOK, THERE'S A SLICE OF AMERICAN CHEESE IN THERE:
If you want to become a Mormon, I'll love you anyway. I just want you to be happy.
R. Chast

"And if you'd like your artwork displayed please include a brief bio."

"Those D's are misleading."

"This is humiliating. Couldn't you drop me a block from school?"

"Derek's sneakers were made in Malaysia. Can anyone show us where Malaysia is?"

THE CRUELTY OF SCHOOL SUPPLIES

"I'm sorry, Ms. Greer, but I can't function under this kind of scrutiny."

"*Mister Jackson! You know how I feel about sampling.*"

"*Please remind your mom and dad that it's a parent-teacher conference, not a parent-teacher-attorney conference.*"

SCHOOL CLOSINGS
OF THE FUTURE

September 11-20: BACK-TO-SCHOOL BREATHER

October 11-18: COLUMBUS WEEK

November 1-20: FALL RECESS

November 25-30: THANKSGIVING

December 1-31: CHRISTMAS/HANUKKAH MONTH

January 7-23: WINTER BREAK

All of February: PRESIDENTS' MONTH

March 9-20: PRE-SPRING BREATHER

April 5-30: EASTER VACATION

May 11-23: MAY DAYS

June 2: LAST DAY OF SCHOOL

R. Chast

"You were kept after school to review multiplication
and division. This is not a date."

"Here's the deal, Josh—these two gentlemen want to turn
that note you passed in homeroom into a movie."

"If nothing else, school has prepared me for a lifetime of backpacking."

"It's one thing for the National Commission to comment on the quality of teaching in our schools. It's another thing entirely for you to stand up and call Mr. Costello a yo-yo."

"I don't have my homework, Miss Flynn—my parents forgot to do it."

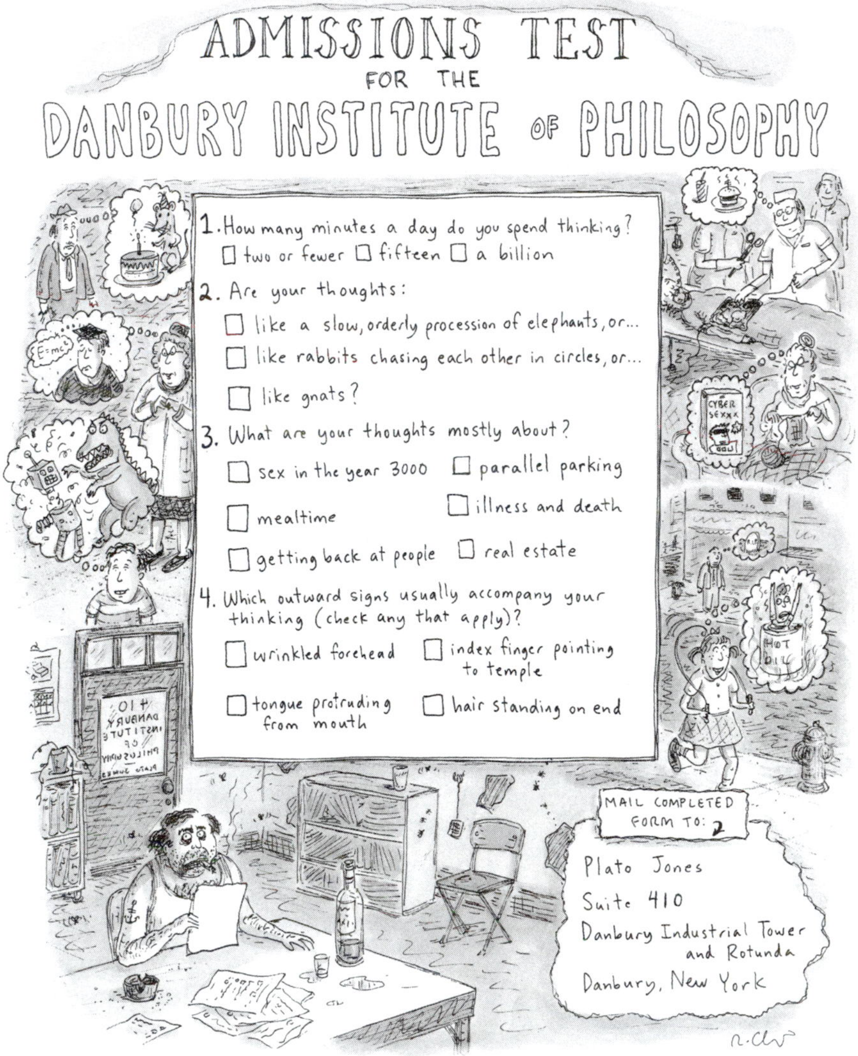
ADMISSIONS TEST
FOR THE
DANBURY INSTITUTE OF PHILOSOPHY
1. How many minutes a day do you spend thinking?
☐ two or fewer ☐ fifteen ☐ a billion
2. Are your thoughts:
☐ like a slow, orderly procession of elephants, or...
☐ like rabbits chasing each other in circles, or...
☐ like gnats?
3. What are your thoughts mostly about?
☐ sex in the year 3000
☐ parallel parking
☐ mealtime
☐ illness and death
☐ getting back at people
☐ real estate
4. Which outward signs usually accompany your thinking (check any that apply)?
☐ wrinkled forehead
☐ index finger pointing to temple
☐ tongue protruding from mouth
☐ hair standing on end
MAIL COMPLETED FORM TO:
Plato Jones
Suite 410
Danbury Industrial Tower and Rotunda
Danbury, New York
R. Chast

"Maybe it's not a wrong answer—maybe it's just a different answer."

"What I Did on My Summer Vacation: A Mystical Journey of Sexual Awakening."

"Your daughter is a pain in the ass."

"O.K., Willy, drag yourself to the table and collapse in despair. Enter Biff."

SIPRESS

"When people say 'Do the math,' is this the kind of thing they're referring to?"

"'Giant Sequoias'—with apologies to the Encyclopaedia Britannica."

"*This is where I come to unwind.*"

"'No More School: A Dream Unfulfilled,' by Howard Willocoski."

"She's utterly lacking in group integration."

"*I* ate my homework."

"What does he know, and how long will he know it?"

B. Smaller

"Keep your eyes on your own screen."

"I'm taking my voucher and going to circus school."

"Being a scientist is going to be a lot easier than I thought."

"*Before I read about my summer vacation, I'd like to ask that all pagers, beepers, and cell phones be turned off.*"

*"Today we're going to explore in paint how we feel
when we're picked up late from preschool."*

"The title of my science project is 'My Little Brother: Nature or Nurture.'"

"The innocence seems forced."

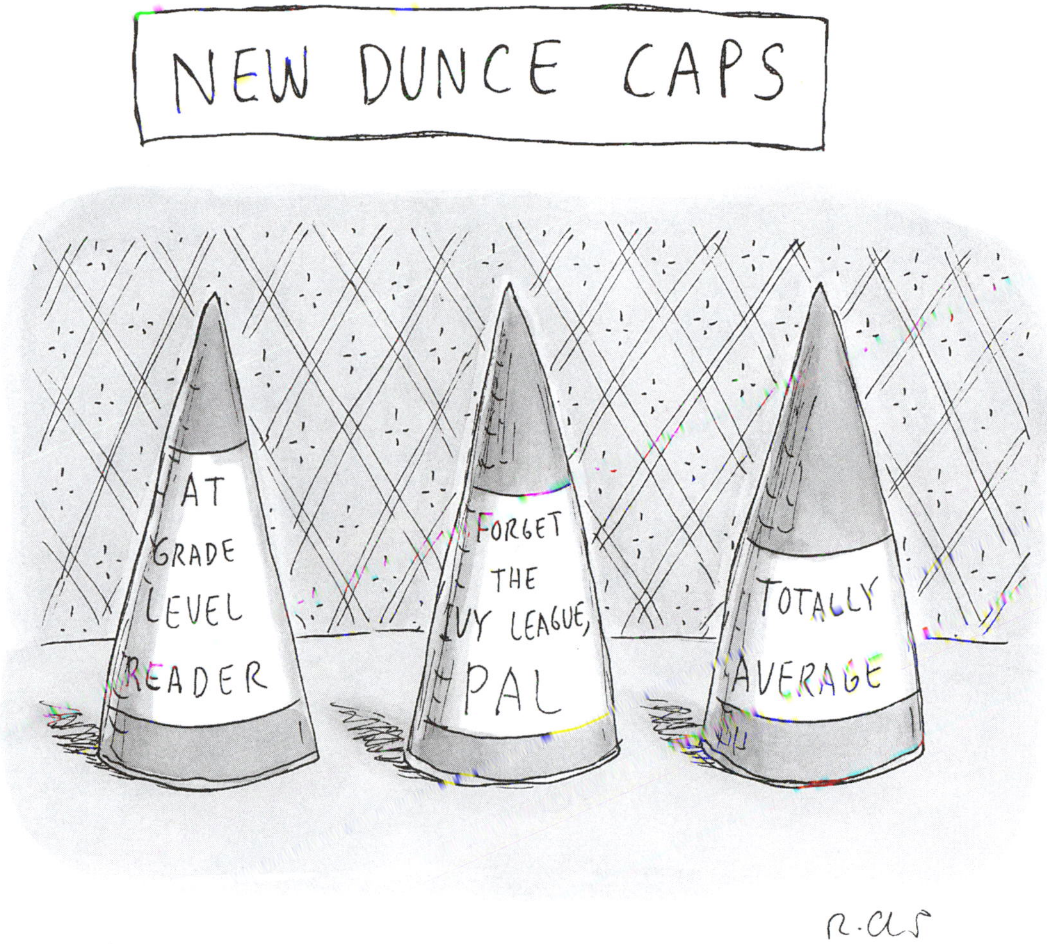
NEW DUNCE CAPS
AT GRADE LEVEL READER
FORGET THE IVY LEAGUE, PAL
TOTALLY AVERAGE

"I'm the only survivor from last semester—what do I win?"

"It may be wrong, but it's how I feel."

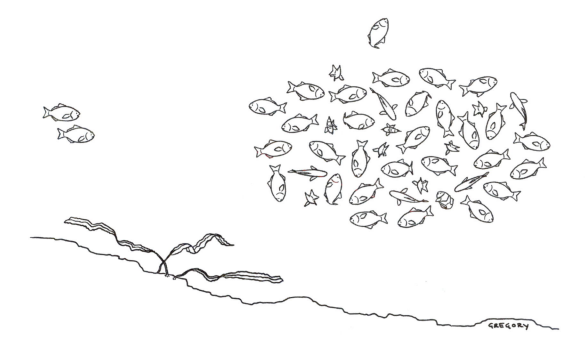

"I believe that's a Montessori school."

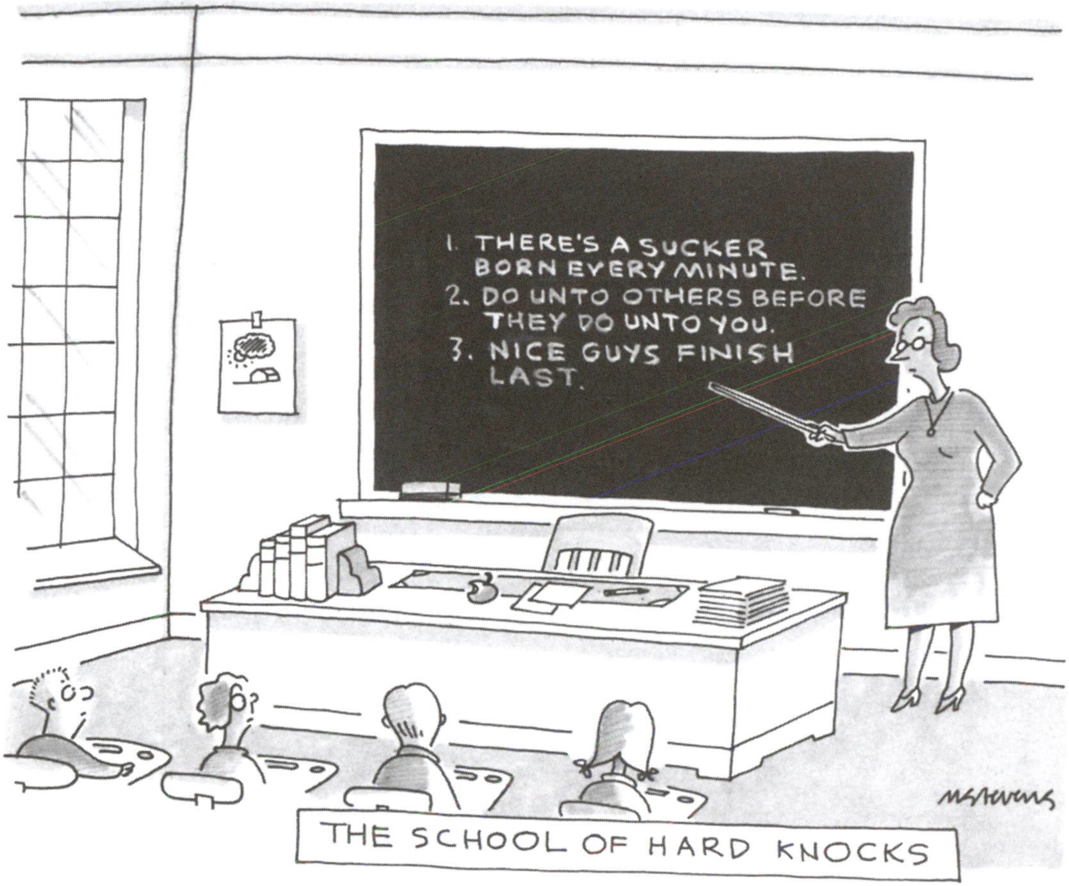
1. THERE'S A SUCKER BORN EVERY MINUTE.
2. DO UNTO OTHERS BEFORE THEY DO UNTO YOU.
3. NICE GUYS FINISH LAST.
THE SCHOOL OF HARD KNOCKS

"If I had *my* way we wouldn't let *any* kids in!"

"I thought it was pretty good, for a book."

"*I pledged allegiance yesterday.*"

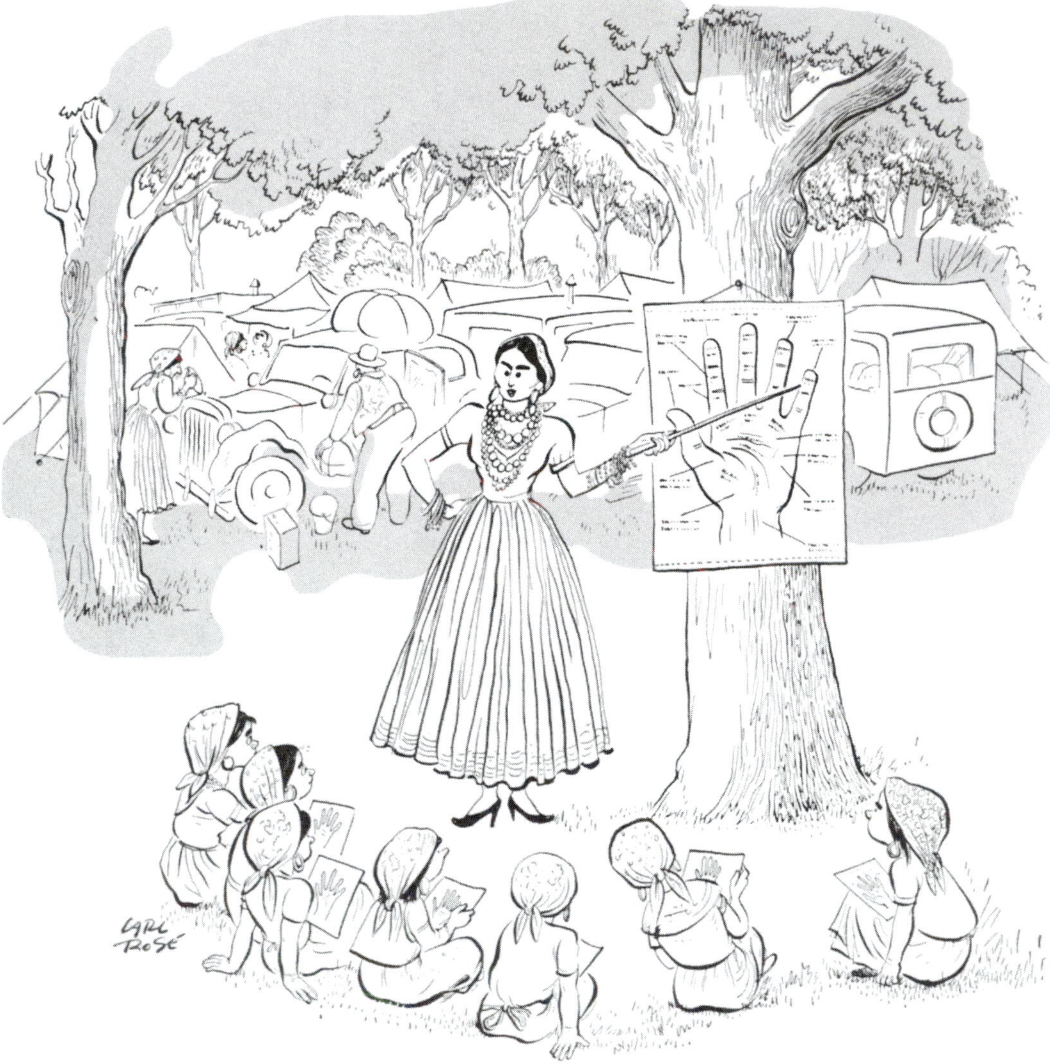
CARL ROSE

"*And that's how ya clean a deer!*"

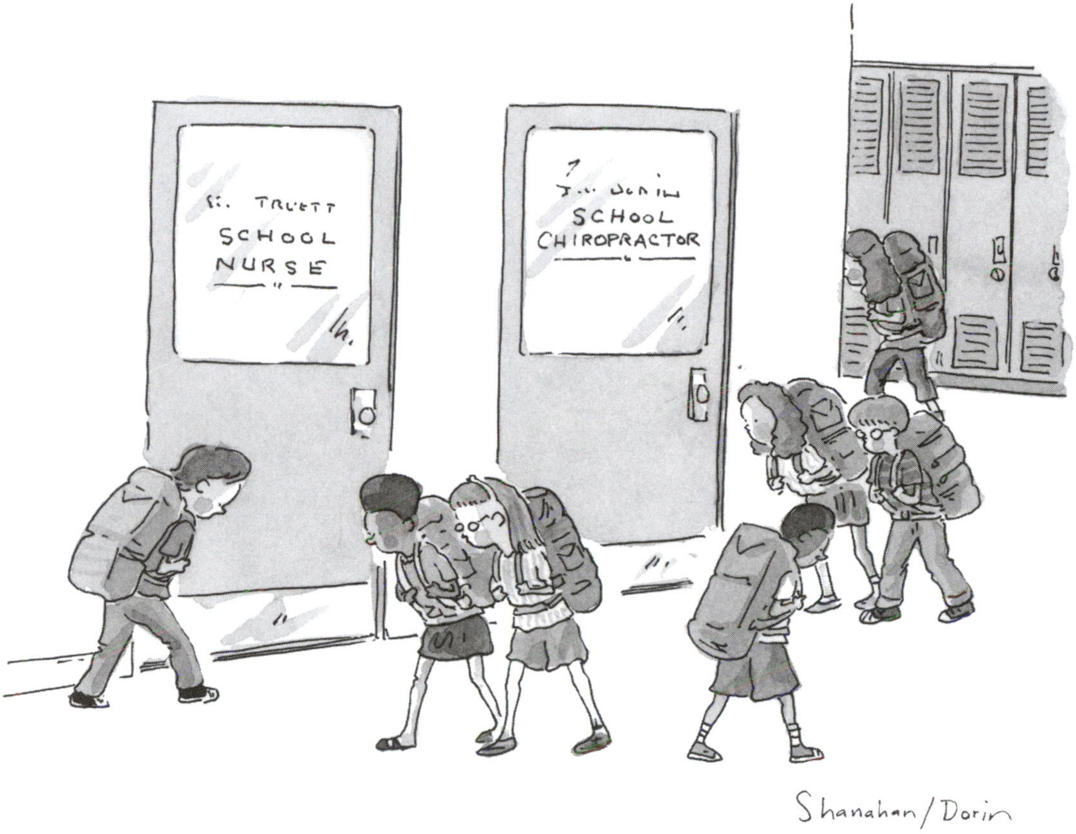
SCHOOL
NURSE
SCHOOL
CHIROPRACTOR
Shanahan/Dorin

"My composition is called 'Mrs. Torrence Is a Big Fat Idiot.'"

"Do you get overtime for this, Miss Marble?"

"Well, it was sort of like a cook-out."

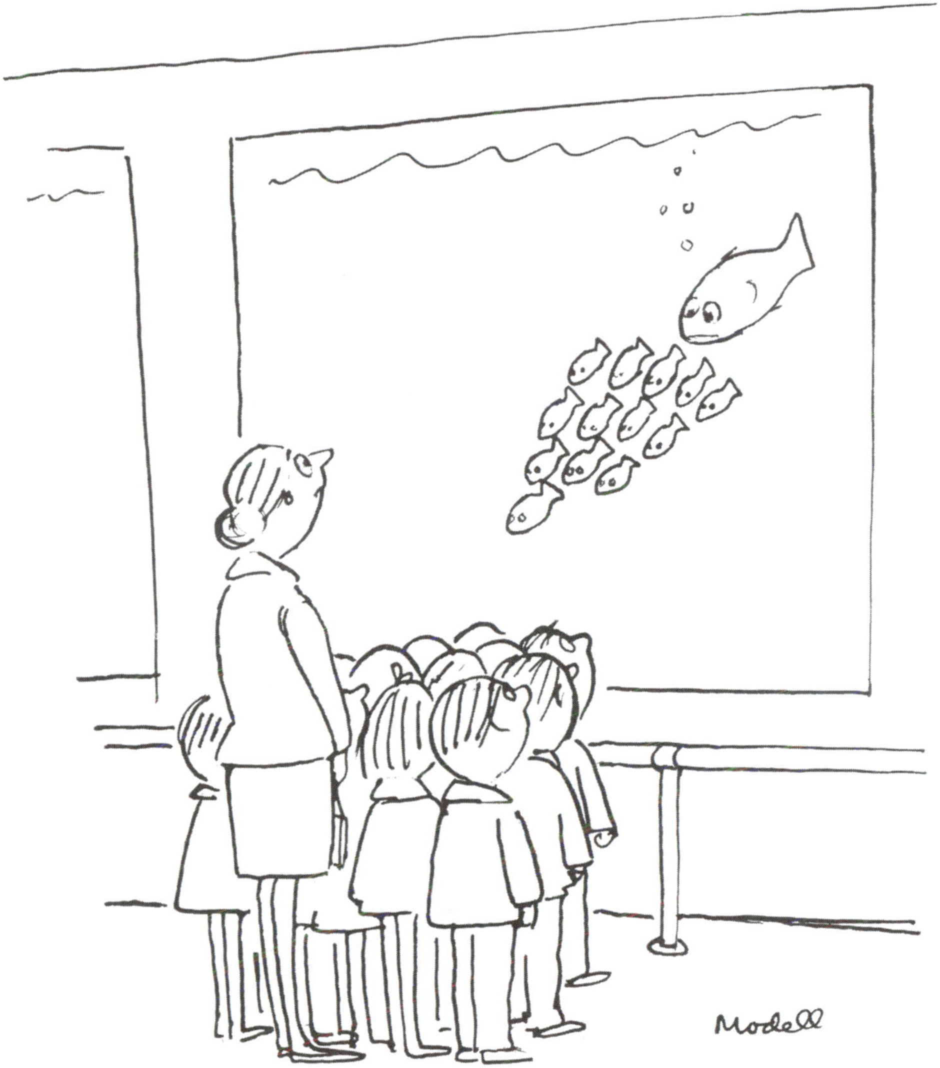
Modell

"The first one to fall asleep gets today's competitive-edge award."

"And another way to help the economy would be to boost teachers' salaries."

"Today's lecture is on loyalty."

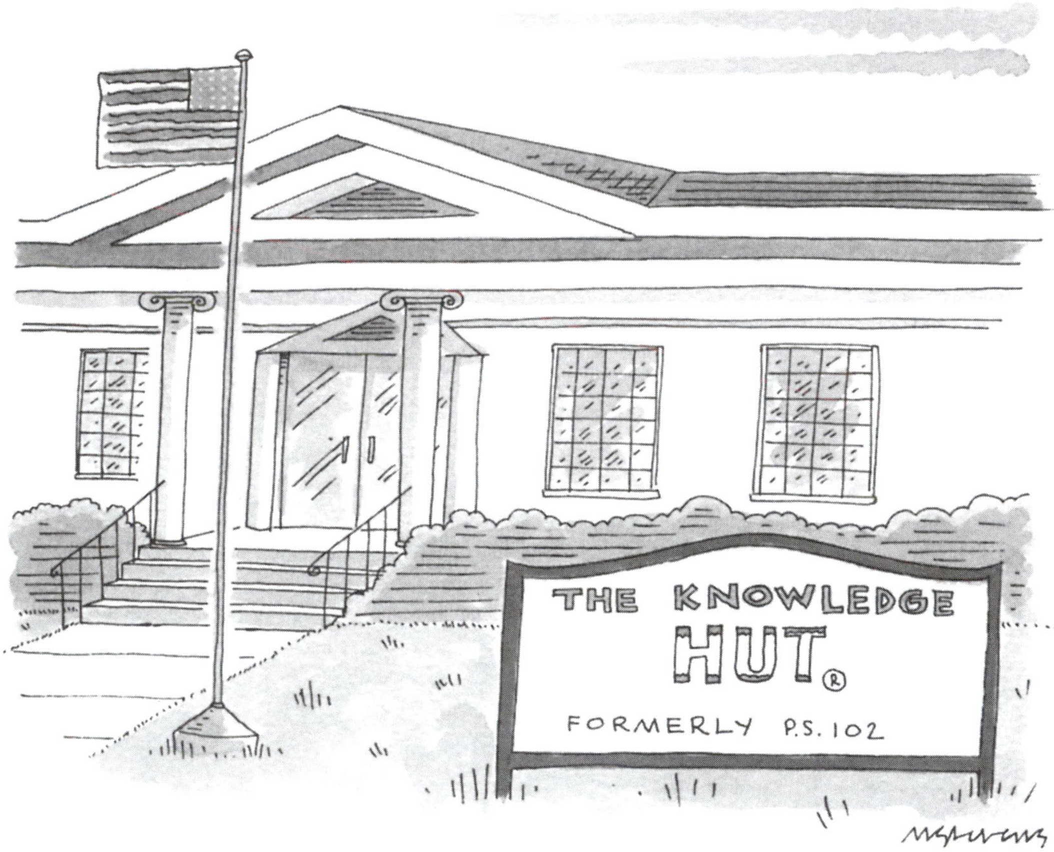
THE KNOWLEDGE
HUT®
FORMERLY P.S. 102

INDEX OF ARTISTS

Wait!
The laughs don't stop there!

Check out these other hilarious collections from

Bloomberg
PRESS

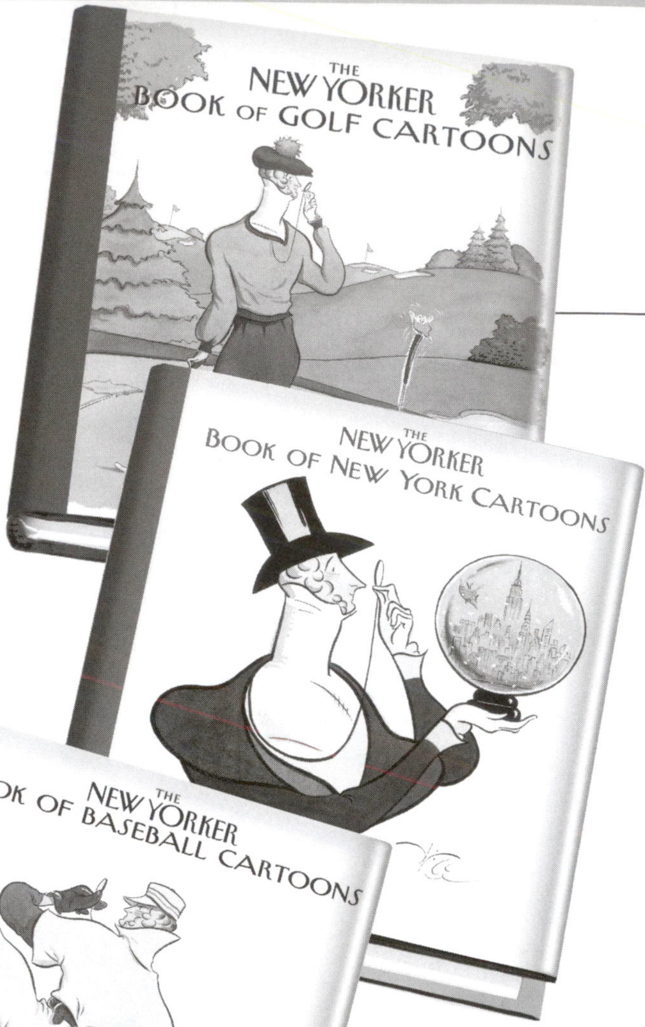
THE NEW YORKER BOOK OF GOLF CARTOONS
THE NEW YORKER BOOK OF NEW YORK CARTOONS

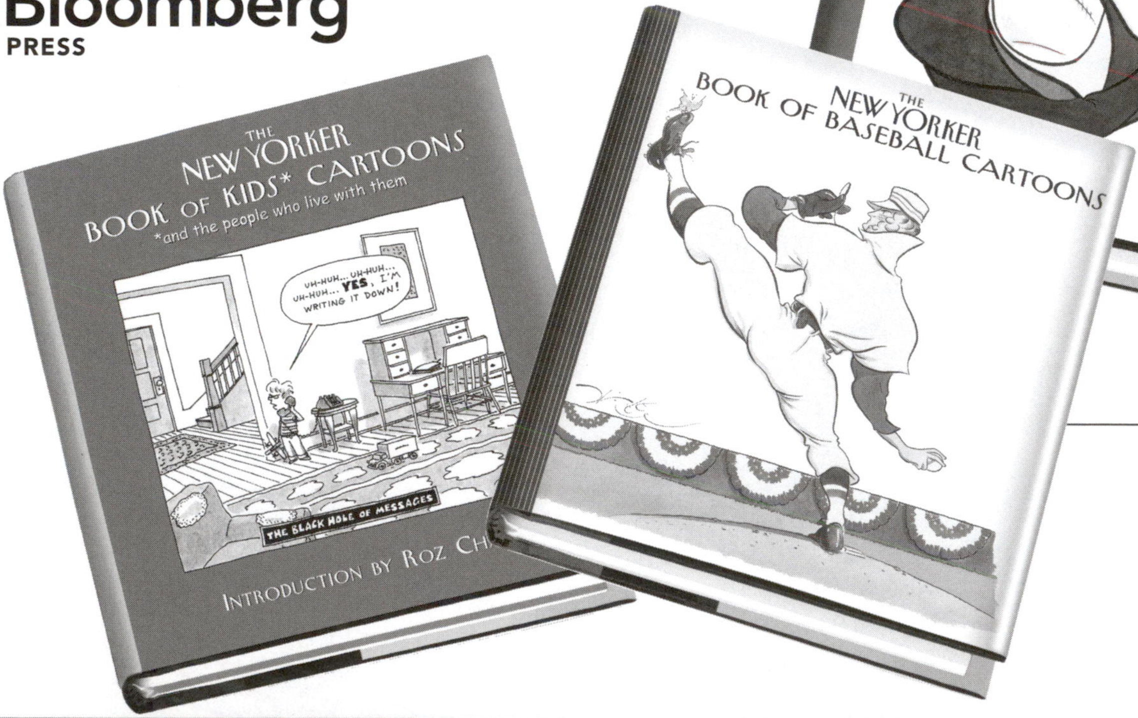
THE NEW YORKER BOOK OF KIDS* CARTOONS
*and the people who live with them
UH-HUH... UH-HUH... UH-HUH... YES, I'M WRITING IT DOWN!
THE BLACK HOLE OF MESSAGES
INTRODUCTION BY ROZ CH
THE NEW YORKER BOOK OF BASEBALL CARTOONS